C000056639

WHERE DO I GO FROM HER?

A JOURNEY FROM LOVE TO LOSS TO LOVE

By

JOHN LEE

WHERE DO I GO FROM HER?

A JOURNEY FROM LOVE TO LOSS TO LOVE

JOHN LEE

Teitelbaum Publishing

ISBN: 978-1-7326485-9-3

Dedicated

To

Kathy Lee McClelland

Sister, Confidant, and Friend

JOHN LEE

ACKNOWLEDGMENTS

In the beginning there was the wrong word. My former assistant, Kat Hrdina, not only supported me by listening to every word I would read to her on so many mornings, but she also helped me with the title of this project. When I told her I would title the book —Where Do I Go From Here —she heard a different and better title, "Did you say it is Where Do I Go From Her?"

"No," I said, "but I will now! Thank you, Kat."

My deepest gratitude goes to Robert Teitelbaum and Teitelbaum Publishing for his labors of love and continued support of my work.

I want to thank Stuart Smith for his talent and time with regards to formatting and printing and much more.

I can't thank my creative friend and former wife, Susan Lee, enough for her beautiful cover.

So much deep appreciation goes to my sister and assistant, Kathy Lee McClelland, who kept supporting me to finish this book.

I appreciate all of you my dear readers, workshop participants, clients and friends (I hope you know who you are) for over three decades of support.

I love you all.

JOHN LEE

PREFACE

When we were gullible kids we actually thought if we dug hard enough, long enough and deep enough we'd come out in China. So, we kept digging. When we were teenagers, we gullible kids thought if we wanted to be in a band badly enough it didn't really matter that no one knew how to play an instrument. When we went to college, we gullible kids actually thought we could marry the captain of the team or the head majorette if they could just get past the fact that we weren't as beautiful as they. When we got married, we gullible kids actually thought we could stay in love forever, but as it turned out digging a hole in the back yard was really more do-able after all compared to separating, divorcing, and then surviving and moving forward and love again.

J.L.

JOHN LEE

∞

"I love what I do not have. You are so far..."

Pablo Naruda

It seems to be a fact that loving is so short and forgetting is so long. That's all I need to say most days.

When she first told me about her need for divorce, I left my body, hovering, clinging to the ceiling certain I'd come back down. Now the days have passed; the months have passed, and I try to re-inhabit my body and make my soul catch up with the fact that we send pictures of our cats and dogs to each other through email, with fewer words between us—a text here and there—and sadness becomes sorrow.

Yesterday my young assistant, Kat, said: "What is the difference between sadness and sorrow?"

I said, I've never been asked that question, nor have I felt the need to distinguish the two.

Sadness is an emotion that comes naturally, and if one allows, it goes and then it comes again as life dictates, whereas now, right now, it would seem I am in a permanent state of sorrow that will be less, greater, even greater, and less again, but at this moment feels like a river that will never make it to the sea.

Sadness is as transient as joy, lasts as long as laughter or fear and then disappears altogether with the new arrival of things—good news, a promotion, a book deal, a new love—but sorrow is four seasons long; it is the constant backdrop for the play that continues though the settings, characters, and time change.

Sadness is, "She's gone," and sorrow is, "She's not coming back," and this is seen everywhere you look, felt every time you see the candleholder you bought together, the painting you picked out to hang in the living room of your cottage, and felt every time any song from Bach to Beatles is played, no matter how sunny and warm the spring day is. Sadness is seeing doors shut. Sorrow is seeing them sealed. But sadness and sorrow can become the creators of a new life – with time and telling the truth about the fact that I lost myself.

∞

I was a fairly sturdy man when we first met. While I wasn't at the top of my game or a huge success in my field, there was some money in the bank in spite of years and years of one bad decision after another.

Pretending I was king of the road took its toll. My extreme efforts to act the part of a fool, an extrovert, a prince, led to extreme alcoholism and two midnight rushes to emergency rooms. Bruised and battered from the climb up the ladder of success and the fall down the stairs in our home, then finally the DUI, and then later the unexpected, unbelievable, out-of-nowhere (except my genetic pool/swamp) came the heart event, and then another one of a different kind, then another one, and another one.

She was creative, brilliant, soft, feminine, and beautiful. I've been with several hard women, not to mention hard men; that was one reason I was so attracted to her. I'd had the shit kicked out of me by the time I was nine by a dad who thought it would make me as hard a man as his dad had made him, so I wanted a soft-landing field for this Puer—the Latin for Eternal

Boy. But if she would ever describe herself as hard it was in very large part my making. Who wouldn't develop a crustacean shell after bankruptcy, alcoholism, being left alone and lonely while I was on the road 200 days a year? Add to this my declining income, triple bypass, and a couple of knee operations, would it be to anyone's surprise if she was suffering from compassion fatigue?

∞

I woke this morning to the sound of my alarm clock in real time and in dream time. Just as it was telling me to get up, I was dreaming I was crawling up stairs (probably the same ones I fell down years ago), and my mother and father were standing there in this dream looking at me, and all I could say is, "How did I get here?" and "I can't wake up."

That says it all for anyone who has visited this strange, nightmarish land place called Divorce Land. How did I get here? It has been three months now since she asked me to, as we used to say in the deep South, "split the quilts." I don't speak the language; I don't know the customs or the culture of the divorced, and I'm damn sure not ready for Match.com, E-harmony, Zoosk, and certainly not Tinder. I can't wrap my head around it all; so, I stare out the windows a lot, looking at this new world that is barren, empty, meaningless—and that's on a good day. On bad days, I pull the covers over my greying head.

Kissing her and the marriage and the dream of the future goodbye is a kind of torture only the divorced ones know. For many of us divorced, it is the "dream" that has to be grieved and mourned as much as the person we were married to. I don't miss who she's become, but I do miss the very kind and maybe the best friend I've ever had and perhaps ever will have.

∞

Surely you remember the kissing? The long, tender, tough, searching, passionate, hour-long kisses? Remember how they became obligatory pecks to say good morning, goodnight, or goodbye? I looked like some deranged chicken pecking around for food that wasn't even there.

Oh, the lovemaking, slow, hard, gentle, crashing, consuming, to "How long has it been?" Probably since we started sleeping in separate bedrooms because of my, and then her, snoring, or so we told ourselves and each other so we wouldn't have to face the truth that our marriage was freezing, as was my less-than-up-and-coming libido and career.

Then she hit the hysterectomy ball out of the park—no more mind- and body-numbing periods, no more possibilities of children, and hello menopause, hot flashes, mood changes, irritability, dissatisfaction, and a burning desire for brilliant glowing sex from a man who was watching his star decline as her star kept rising.

∞

"For the more haunted among us, only looking at the past can permit it finally to become past."

Mary Karr

What do ex-cons, alcoholics, and the divorced all share in common, at least the ones of us that are still left? A morbid fascination with the past and where we went wrong—the DUIs and jail, and the gallons of booze that floated our beer bellies to jail. We tear apart the past like a dog with a new chewy toy. We shake it fiercely like it was really alive; we tear at its fake fur; we go for the squeaky part first and then tear out the stuffing until we've annihilated the truth of things with our animal teeth and bad memories, and we still don't get a satisfying answer.

We talk to therapists, friends, priests, God, the Devil, until only our furry friends like dogs, cats, and horses will listen as we deconstruct and over-analyze the sagging of marriage and divorce.

∞

Early mid-life woman, late mid-life man; in other words, she grew up and I grew old. You know that thing that flashes every other day or so across your face and your wrinkled eyes is called our life; well, she saw her life floating by, then soaring by, while mine was zooming by.

I was old on the day I was born. People have told me all my life I was older than my years. Frequently, I was asked if I was my mother's brother. Most of my friends were, and are, five to fifteen to twenty years older than me.

She was raised, encouraged, and supported to always look ten years younger than she really was, and that lasted until her mid-forties.

Many a time I was asked if she is my daughter. The first time was right before my first colonoscopy; the second was at the movie theatre.

She went from her high school to local college, lived at home, went to work (occasionally) for her father, ushering both her father and mother into adulthood while he was drinking. That did put some years on her.

Me, I'd been working since I was twelve in my dad's dirty machine shop, and before that, on the farm with no indoor plumbing and a very cold, dark, wasp- and spider-ridden outhouse. No, I'm not as old as it sounds; we were just poor there for a pretty good while. While she had maids, nannies, and cooks to comfort and soothe her, I had cigarettes, caffeine, and carelessness—oh, and alcohol by thirteen—to soothe my soul because by then I'd given up on any kind of spirit except those that come out of a bottle of bourbon or an Old Milwaukee or Pabst beer can. I knew nothing about self-soothing until my late thirties and she taught me a good deal more about it in my forties. When she was restless and couldn't sleep, she half-awake, would hold her arm in the air and with her other hand stroke it gently like it was a sleepy cat, and then in just a few moments go back sound asleep, while me, the eternal insomniac, would take the remote control or a drink or Ambien and be continually frustrated that she knew something I didn't. Finally, one morning I asked her what was the arm stroking about? "Oh, that? That is what my nanny would do when I was young and couldn't sleep."

$$\infty$$

We don't know when "Mid-Life" or its accompanying crisis comes and goes anymore. It used to be around forty or so. Now it is … well, we don't know. What I am sure of is that it still exists. I've been through a couple of them myself. I also know that friends, clients, wives and husbands, get in this boat with holes or are devoured by it like that shark in the movie *Jaws*. It is a time when we most assuredly "need a bigger boat."

I also know while folks are trying to recover from their confrontation with Reality, they make huge rash and regressed decisions, thinking this stage is a permanent one, unlike childhood or adolescence. So the man tears off his necktie and tosses it into the garbage, cashes in his 401k, kisses his wife and children goodbye, buys a 1965 Mustang (preferably a convertible), builds a cabin in the woods of Alabama or Oregon, and dates the waitress at the local greasy spoon. Finally, he wakes up one cold morning, realizing just what he's done ... "and find yourself in another part of the world ... and you may ask yourself, well how did I get here?" (Talking Heads)

What do women do? I don't know. I know what some do as they see their life passing before them. They want their power back or want it for the first time. They read, write, keep journals, talk to women friends, go online for a Mid-Life Women's support group, screw younger men, or older ones, climb the ladder that fell on their husbands, have a 401k, and kick some butt.

However, they too, seem to make impulsive decisions, choices, and selections while in this temporary stage. Rather than negotiate it and work through it, they ask for divorce and move on in ways that most men cannot do. I've known more than a few women who don't seem to need or want closure because most, by the time of signing the papers, have been closed up a long time before. Tears come abundantly; rage comes and goes, and then it gets quiet in there, real quiet, and then—I don't know, or, as T.S. Eliot said in his poem, *Portrait of A Lady*, be "...prepared for all the things to be said, or left unsaid..."

∞

It has been some months now since she asked for the divorce. Yesterday, I realized that almost two hours had passed that were not haunted by the ghost of marriage past. The specter of what was and what wasn't haunts me at night, pulling my memory into deep darkness and I almost drown in my own cold sweats, and sometimes I think I hear her there in my room calling my name – "John."

I rise somehow the next morning covered in remorse and regret, wishing I could have only done the things she wanted and needed without losing and betraying myself even further.

You see, her testosterone was rising while mine was descending like an ancient mercury-filled thermometer. My estrogen was informing my decision to be taken care of just once, just for a while, and she gladly accommodated, having stayed at home all those years being much less than she could be, and thanks to fundamental Christianity, kept her world, when she was young, mostly chaste, and extremely inexperienced.

I, on the other hand, mostly in my rebellious youth which lasted well into my thirties—well, let's just say I'd been around the block more times than a Jehovah's Witness. I seduced and was seduced, and glad to be and do so. By the time her libido kicked in, my pilot light was almost out. When it would ignite, it wouldn't sufficiently heat a small room much less a beautiful woman.

This was especially true after my heart attack and triple bypass surgery. After that, I felt weak and vulnerable, overly cautious whether I was driving a car or wanting to park my full emotional and sexual life in the parking place of her arms.

The fragility in me, one I'd never known, was costing us as I went on the road less and less, and she entered the work force more and more, until the day came when she was the primary breadwinner.

I thought, "Yes," I'll be graceful. I'll receive for a while. I have done my therapeutic homework; I attended men's conferences with Robert Bly, Sam Keen; I will dance with my declining income."

I didn't. I stumbled, fell flat on my face, and got smaller in her and my own eyes when I couldn't escape from the mirrors on the wall, "asking who is the fairest of them all?" "Not you, you paid member of AARP."

∞

You know how people say, "It's not about the money?" Well, it's always about the money. In two days, we will cut another cord made out of plastic and the IRS. We're meeting at our bank to "separate" our finances. She will pay for this; I'll pay for that, and we'll both pay dearly for the holes that will be left in our separate bank accounts and individual souls.

I've never done this before and neither has she. There won't be any haggling because she knows I'll acquiesce, being the one who will receive a monthly alimony check until such a time that I don't need them.

It doesn't matter a tinker's damn that I was the primary breadwinner (wheat-free, gluten-free, preservative-free) for all those years. The cut issued by the branch manager will be precise, surgically performed with no anesthesia. She will patch it up with a hug, a kiss on the cheek, and say how sorry she is, and she will mean it. This all will be done with little or no malice or meanness in her, just a lot of self-preservation. Me, I'll feel like I've been in castration surgery for days until the shock of it all wears off and the fears subside.

∞

Memory and Desire, go to your separate corners, and you shall never meet in the center, and be sure to remove your wedding rings. What I desire to remember are only the good times we shared, admittedly acknowledging that there were far less than there should have been, given I was working all the time.

My father taught, or more accurately indoctrinated me, in his addictive work ethic. He put my dyslexic, acne-pock-marked face to work in his dirty,

9

seldom-profitable machine shop, which didn't help my already growing angry disposition. That is where my addiction to work began as a numbing device to relieve the pain of my childhood. I've been working ever since. The poet Robert Bly has a few lines in a poem that are so relevant I memorized them. "Think that someone is going to give you something large, or tell you that you have been forgiven, or that you don't have to work all the time, or if you lie down no one will die." I've tried to exorcise Dad and it from my system. Perhaps I need an old-fashioned Priest after all. While poetry may let you befriend your demons, it does little to make them totally disappear.

Her father, when he was not drinking, allowed her to "come and go talking about Michelangelo" like the fine ladies in Eliot's poem, *Love Song of J. Alfred*. Her father's period of alcoholism forced her into a care-taking role—after all, she had two infants to take care of—her mom and dad. But work was optional due to his ability to be "functional" and profitable.

Take one workaholic man and add one princess who brings along her parents'-imposed pea to put under the bed and what do you have? Ultimately it's a lot of distance between memory and desire, worker bee and Queen. Truthfully, it was harder on both of us than it should have been.

∞

Here I sit in my temporary, over-priced house in Austin. There's the leather chair her mother and father gave us. We disliked it so much we'd sit on it only when we would let our three dogs climb on board and roughhouse. I always said I didn't like it, but I got it in the Great Divide.

Over there is the bed her mom and dad gave us. She said it was too hard so she would sleep on the softer one in our bedroom. That became hers and I got the one in the "spare room," and there I slept month after month in the darkness fearing what was coming or going.

I got the table; she got the recliner; I got, she got, I got, she got, and now we proceed to meet at the IRS at eleven o'clock for another attempt to divide the responsibilities and the deep pain as we drive one more nail into the coffin of our sixteen-year marriage. Maybe we should all agree to close the doors on the word "divorce" and just say, when friends ask, "I hear you lived, just barely, through the Great Divide?" Isn't that like The Great Depression? No, there wasn't enough stuff back then to divide, so most stayed married or killed each other, at least that's true where I'm from.

∞

There are always at least four people in any marriage, or at least there were in ours. There was me, and then this other "I." There was her, and then her other "I."

There was the me who wanted to stay married for life and would tolerate just about any unwelcomed behavior, and then there is the "I" who knew it wasn't working for a long time, who was saying loud and clear, though no one was listening, "and this, too, shall end."

This "I" was always the smarter of the two. Her "I" was smarter. They both knew what to do and not to do if we really wanted the marriage to continue.

Me and Her wouldn't listen to these deeper, more intelligent voices, and so here Me and "I" sit in a black recliner (that her father gave us) trying to write about Me and "I," She and her "I," knowing all four of us are sad, angry, lonely, confused, hurt, and mourning the fact that some part of us did not want to be married anymore and so that part has been heard, though both parts of me still feel, and will feel for a long time, if not forever, that I and me are still married to Her.

∞

"...This is the way the world ends

Not with a bang but with a whimper."

T.S. Eliot, *Hollow Man*

This is the way our marriage ended, no "bangs," nothing physical, no shouting, no name calling, but almost daily I cry and whimper like yesterday.

Yesterday, I went to her new apartment to retrieve our three animal companions. She kept the two cats because of the space, and I got the dogs because the house I rented had a big, fenced-in yard. And in truth, we are equally bonded to them. I sorely miss the twenty-one-year-old white cat, Casper, and dark as night, Squeaky cat, who is angry at everyone. My Ex longs for Foxy, the Giant Alaskan Malamute, Bella the wiener mix with lab, and Luna, our very own Benjy dog that we got from the shelter when she was six months old.

Packing them up in the van that I got because the Volvo can't accommodate our 140-pound Malamute, I cried. No, I whimpered, not wanting her to see how still torn up I can be every time we split the family.

For you that have children that spend weekends, weeks, or parts of summer vacations away, I can't imagine the pain you must go through if it is this heartbreaking with a family of furry ones, how deep it must feel. "This is the way the world ends; this is the way the world ends."

∞

Talk about the country bumpkin crashing a party at the posh country club—that was me. Her pedigree compared to my "mutt-ness."

She was a princess—the first time I was to view her in her private world of home, you could see how she'd been raised and then when I visited her and her family's home, I knew I was not their kind. They weren't the super-rich, but they were very wealthy—I with my too-long unkempt beard, eyebrows too untamed, hair growing a little too freely out my ears said it all.

The whole house was filled with paintings and pictures of her and her artwork. The painting right as you walked in the front door was a very erotic, sexual pose of her that I couldn't believe any parent would want to flaunt.

On my side of the family, we all have made our homes in trailer parks at one time or another, only to upscale as we got older to doublewides and cinderblock houses, and finally modest, lower middle-class suburban houses. "Etiquette" sounded more like "Have you 'et yet?" She had plenty for the both of us and then some.

This was our coming together; this was just one of many reasons to part. She wanted a long-lasting tea party, and I liked coffee. She loves carpet, I love hardwood floors; she likes new; I like very little that isn't a hundred years old; she had her teeth whitened and capped; I wore old baseball caps. I liked to work in the yard. She couldn't, wouldn't, and didn't.

God, we were so different. Opposites do attract and, in our case, made each other laugh our heads off—at least we had a comedy club marriage with lots of humor which was probably the number one reason we lasted as long as we did.

But opposites also wear each other down and the laughter comes less and less, and now she lives in a new, carpeted apartment and I live in a wood-floored house that is at least older than I am, and I miss her and carpet so much as I write this.

∞

When anything is dead, it should be buried, and that goes along for marriages, "If it is dead, bury it."

I seem to have misplaced my shovel, and even if I knew where it was, the ground is cold and hard here on the mountain and frozen just like my old heart. Where would I bury this marriage if the Spring softens the earth and my resolve to put it to its final resting spot? In a memoir, a screen play? Perhaps a work of fiction, then I could give it the ending I preferred. Maybe I could put the marriage corpse next to the grave of our giant white Alaskan Malamute, Mr. Mio. We raised him together and buried him together seven years ago. She loved him as much as I. I could dig a spot next to the giant who was gentle and cover the old and write about it with more tears and then go have a reception, a celebration that it all has run its course. But of course, that day has not come or been earned yet.

∞

"I receive alimony." There, I've said it: Alimony, acrimony, allegory, agony.

I receive the money which causes some acrimony, the whole act of doing so would make for a good allegory of the King who was dethroned by his own wife, and the agony that follows no longer being able to wear the crown which was made of garlands and flowers, woven together by his Queen he loved so much and who had once loved him.

How can a man swallow his pride and take such a bitter pill? Many do it with beer, whiskey, porn, accumulating more money, and getting another Princess to be watched as she turns into a Queen.

I have no such helpers, being a dyed-in-the-wool recovering alcoholic. My body has taken on the pain of the divorce. It makes me sick to my stomach; it makes me needy and my knee replacement won't allow me to bend down on them without more pain and ask God to forgive me of all the ways I missed the mark in the marriage. My old hip keeps me from acting "hip" (as if I could at this stage of life). My back is bent, shoulders to the floor; these all say I am carrying way too much guilt, shame, anger, and sadness.

I need to exercise, exorcise the pain in my arthritic, geometrically increasing amount of hurt every time we see each other for some mundane, inane, insane talk about taxes or bank accounts or credit cards, or when she comes to pick up the dogs that keep us bound together after all else is gone.

The half-hearted hugs, a limp kiss on the cheek hello or goodbye, reserved for acquaintances, party guests, and parting kisses all the while thanking her for the alimony.

∞

And what about the vows? "For better or worse, in sickness and in health, until death do us part." One of us meant them. I guess that was me. I guess she meant them at the time. See, the problem is if you stay together for a pretty long time, you find yourself married to many women or men.

I watched my wife slowly, but too quickly for my slow Appalachian ways, become someone else three or four times during our sixteen years. Ingénue to Princess, to Attempted Mother, to Worker Bee, to owning her own company, from city girl to country girl, and then she became a broken hearted, but excellent businesswoman and grand creator of novels, and finally, a single, divorced, middle-aged woman searching for her disappeared life wanting something I couldn't provide.

She wanted to go places I'd already been and could not go again, and so the fifth or sixth wife has forgotten those vows, but not the one she made to herself somewhere during these transitions; I was not present enough to see, and that was to become the person she was meant to be and be happy for doing so.

∞

I can count on one hand the number of days that we didn't talk to one another for nearly sixteen years. No matter where the road and work took me—Australia, Austin, Chicago, London—we talked at least once a day, sometimes twice or more. Now we talk maybe once a week. It is a withdrawal worse than coming off alcohol or drugs, and probably heroin and cocaine since almost no one uses those to ease the pain every day for sixteen years.

Now we text our thoughts, feelings, and facts to each other maybe once a day, sometimes only every other day. We've achieved a monosyllabic divorce, only a few words in a text to express a world of sadness, loneliness, and missing.

Those few texts will soon disappear or decline to one a week, then one a month, and then none. But no one tells you how to prepare to go from talking to not talking virtually overnight.

I miss hearing about her day, telling her about mine, sharing with her some stupid thing the dogs did on our daily walk. I miss hearing her physical complaints and speaking out loud about my own. I miss talking and listening, so I write and write, but it's just not the same.

I almost never give advice unless someone asks. In forty years as a counselor and therapist, I've found people don't like it and usually ignore it if it is unsolicited. John Steinbeck said, "People don't want advice; they want affirmation."

But here it goes anyway. Perhaps take it more as a suggestion. Get rid of all your old, worn-out, holey t-shirts and underwear. Don't spend more than two hours during a weekday in your sweatpants, no more than three hours on the weekend. Don't wear flip-flops anywhere, not at home, not to Walmart, and not even to McDonalds. They are only meant for the beach and public showers.

Do you watch a lot less television? There's nothing worth a shit on anyway, and make love more often. Go to the movies and hold hands, pet each other more than you do the cats or dogs. Take long walks in the morning or evening and stop occasionally and look each other in the eyes, and never, ever let your eyes wander when he or she is right there and can see your love and energy leaking out. And when you kiss—really kiss. Reserve the pecks for your grown children, friends, family... You never know which one may be your last.

∞

Pain trumps everything. When bones and body, blood and genes turn on you, the sun can't be seen; love can't be felt; love can't be made, and conversation staggers, stutters, sputters, and then the silence between partners protrudes into every room and every corner of every room and the obligatory marriage chatter is all that remains.

The, "How's your day been?" feels like part of an ongoing interrogation, the asker hoping for a different answer than yesterday.

"Oh, my fibromyalgia has really been acting up."

"Yeah, my knee is killing me."

"My chronic fatigue is wearing me out. Sorry no dinner tonight."

"What about our date night?"

"It will have to be another night," another week, another month, maybe next year, maybe next marriage.

Pain trumps everything and exhaustion is its twin, and love didn't stand a chance to win.

∞

Anger is for getting out of stuck places and grief is for having been in them for so long. My ex-wife got angry, very angry. She got stuck in the mud of marriage, the quicksand of matrimony, the rapidly drying concrete of continuity. She got angry that life, God, Fate, the Universe, betrayed her. Throw in my betrayals—not with other women, but my oath to work, and the world, and she got very angry.

So, she strapped on her female armor, polished and sharpened her sword/tongue, and began cutting me, disrespecting me, talking to me like one would to an unruly teenager or a naughty child. I got angry and withdrew my affection, my feelings, and Eros, and this made her even more angry.

None of this was conscious, intentional, or malicious, but all of this was a preparation for the plywood coffin of our dying marriage. She wanted it to be finished so she and it could rest in peace.

There is no rest during and after a divorce—there is guilt, hindsight, Monday morning quarterbacking, lots of crying over the milk of human kindness that seemed to be spilled between us, and we mostly just tolerated our stuckness until she got angry enough to push us both out of the red mud of a marriage.

∞

As I said, grief is for having been stuck in uncomfortable, incorrect, dysfunctional places, relationships, jobs, or marriages. Grief is the proper human response to loss, transition, changes, and to the things we didn't have and should have been given.

Where's my anger? Still covered, smothered by the immense grief of losing not only my wife, but my best friend, my confidant, my editor, etc., etc.

My sadness wraps around me, enters me, and circulates like my thin blood. My sense that I am experiencing the greatest loss of my adult life is overwhelming me most days. It has laid me down and out, and gutted me like a fish so that I may be cooked by life some more to be made more tender, more helpful, more what? – to make God, the one who loved Job, feel stronger to feed his power-hungry lust?

I get it, God, you give dreams and you take away dreams. You give love and turn it into anger. You are a great giver and a great taker away, God, or maybe you don't have a damn thing to do with any of it. Look, I just got a little angry there for about ten seconds.

∞

"The serious problems in life are never fully solved," says Carl Jung. Boy, did he get that one right. The problem of loving the woman in your mind and the woman sitting across from you at the breakfast table, secretly planning her life after divorce, is hard to endure.

How to love, how to be loved, how to live with another day after day, year after year, decade after decade?

Our forefathers and mothers didn't have to wonder about future decades. In the 1860s, a man's life span was about forty-six and a woman's, forty-eight, but of course, they were married to each other practically right out of the womb. I have great-aunts and great-grandmothers who married at thirteen, fourteen, and fifteen. In Texas there is a law on the books today saying no one under thirteen years old can be married.

Like I've said, if you stay with your spouse for even ten or fifteen years, let alone twenty, thirty, or more, there are so many "hers" and so many "yous" that both must learn to love. And some of our "us-es" during certain periods of our life are just damn near impossible to talk to much less love.

∞

To be sure, I have cried a few buckets of tears having lost my wife, best friend, and confidant. However, many of those tears intermingled with the tears that come from having lost myself—the core me in the marriage. I did things, became things, said things, not done things, and not said things, that years ago I would not abide; that would not have been me.

When I met her, I had a smidgen of self-esteem and self-worth, and thought I knew who I was and what I'd never lose again after working so hard to find.

By the time she announced her readiness to say, "see ya'," I was unsure of myself, my masculinity, my strength, and my basic character. I had let the rough waters of marriage make my small lifeboat sink.

∞

Things change. For example, I held the belief in my thirties and forties that I would, should old age come, just "age gracefully." Bullshit! I've entered into the fall of my life kicking and screaming. Well, more screaming and crying than kicking due to my bad knees.

Bette Davis said it best: "Growing old ain't for sissies." What a sissy I am. I bitch about some pain, soreness, aches, and maladies, and that's just before breakfast.

I eat raw kale. I take every kind of vitamin and supplement known to Western and Eastern man. I take a pill for blood pressure, a pill to keep my arteries from becoming concrete, a pill to ... well, you get the picture. Go take your pills before you forget, and your Miralax; that's very important.

The other part is purely emotional and that is: in my sixties I'm totally invisible. If all the checkout people at Whole Foods were in their twenties or thirties, I could fill up three or four baskets, put a flower in my mouth, and walk out without paying totally unseen. Hell, I can't get forty-somethings to look at my fading baby blues for all the grey in my hair and beard. Invisible, I say! Hear me whimper? I used to roar-ish.

∞

"Each time I see him, he says, 'It is rough' or 'I didn't think it would end like this.'" This is a line from the best journal writer, May Sarton, talking about a friend she goes to see who is dying. I use the same words when my dear friends ask me how it is going, meaning the divorce, my very own small death. For divorce is like death and should be mourned that way. Cover the mirrors, wear Johnny Cash black, or at least an armband, have people bring zucchini casseroles, French bread, and fill the refrigerator with desserts.

That man I was, like that woman she was, has died. The great prophet Mohammad said, "Die before you die." He is talking about death to the ego, death to vanity, death to desire, reputation, wealth, and all the false selves that others and ourselves created to get through the comic/tragic play called the first half of our lives.

Marriage will kill off many of these artificial personas, and divorce will murder a few more. I don't know how folks go through, survive to rise from your graves and marry a second, a third time, even a fourth time. You have to be stronger or extremely stubborn or have found some magical potion to restore your readiness to receive and give to another.

∞

*"The reasons for depression are not so interesting
as the way one handles it, simply to stay alive."*

May Sarton

So, I sit in my solitude, a prisoner of depression, a cellmate to a ticking clock, and let the silence enter my broken heart. I am depressed and have been for a long time. The divorce request has brought me to an invisible state of despair and an obvious look of disrepair. I lost twenty-five pounds—I don't recommend the divorce diet that, for me, included donations from hundreds of chickens and buckets of oatmeal along with gallons of ginger ale because that is all my knotted stomach could force down and keep down. I forgot or didn't care to get my hair cut for the first time in thirty years. My jeans hung on me desperately; my shirts looked like they belonged to a much larger man.

Sarton says, "simply stay alive."

∞

"I think I could turn and live awhile with the animals... They do not sweat and whine about their condition, they do not lie awake in the dark and weep for their sins."

Walt Whitman

And so that is what I do. I have three animal companions and I sit with them or rather they sit with me.

I used to think, when I was a boy and young man, that dogs and cats were only beggars and takers of food and attention and should live outdoors come winter wind, rain, or heat. I have known now for many, many years they come into our lives not to take, but to give the one thing we long for humans to give but can't: unconditional love. They are also God's conduits for healing. Our Malamute lies on my Ex's stomach when she's sick. When I'm sad, she comes to comfort me. When we divorced, they all came as if to say, "do not lie away in the dark and weep for your sins, because you did not sin;" you made mistakes; you missed the mark, and said and did things you shouldn't have. Barking, purring, playing, they make me want to be Whitman and "stand and look at them sometimes half the day long" instead of looking at my old failures.

∞

She's not coming back and that is the way it is. Would I take her back should she ever ask? Would I ask or plead for her to take me back? The answer is a loud, resounding, "No!" Why? Because the worst is almost over. The crying every day is stopping; the urgency to call or be called by friends is lessening. It's been only six months and I would say, "This is what you wanted. This is what you, like Kali the Great Destroyer, set in motion. This is the price you pay, I pay, our pets pay, for your freedom to journey into the unknown, into dating," and me – solitude on a Saturday night.

I'd say, "No, I still love you. You were and are the love of my adult life and you betrayed me with your need to try to capture what you did not get to do in your twenties and thirties due to the harsh way you were raised, but I'm pretty sure what we miss is what we miss, and at fifty, what felt right to say and do at twenty or thirty won't come close to feeling good now." And that's the way my anger says it is.

∞

It's the infant in me that wants her to change her mind and come back. When I was younger and crazy, I would sometimes consciously push a woman I loved away, just so I could see if I could get her to come back. One or two misguided, loving women did, and then I finally succeeded in pushing them away again, and then I'd move on. That was the infant in me pushing his needy mother away then finding out she was the source of life and begging her to return.

This time, these sixteen years later, there was no such infantile need to get her to go away, or, please come back! This time it is only the man who mourns the way a man is supposed to mourn—silently, loudly, in solitude, and surrounded by support. It is the man who knows deep down inside his sinews and soul that she's not coming back and, like I've said before, the woman she is and the man I am are fundamentally incompatible.

"I come back, I shiver in my isolation, and must face again and try to tame the loneliness. The house is no friend when I walk in...my life waiting for me somewhere, asking to be created again..."

May Sarton

Like Sarton, this is how I feel every time I return home after taking or picking up our dogs after their weekend visitation with my ex. "I shiver in my isolation" and begin again the grieving process, fresh and anew, thinking before seeing her with the dogs that I was nearly done.

Sixteen years can't be retrieved, and they can't be grieved in six months. I am taking a full year, maybe more, maybe lots more time to mourn the loss of marriage and rebuild a man—me—from the ground up, from toe to head, to change radically. The poet Wendell Berry says, "What must a man do to be at home in this world?" I ask the same question less eloquently almost every day.

∞

Who will finish my sentences? Who will say, "that is exactly what I was going to say?" Who is going to text me, email me, or better yet, call me at the exact same moment I was about to do so? The answer I have to give for now in my sixties, is probably, no one – at least for a long time to come.

Sixteen, going on seventeen years, you build a psychic intuitive connection. Your thoughts and feelings get transferred by some mysterious current, the dark energy, the Quantum Physics people are talking about. Who knows?

My first white giant Alaskan Malamute, Mio, would sit by the door thirty minutes to an hour before I'd arrive home, having gone to Atlanta for a day or Australia for a month.

It is no wonder my former wife and I developed a similar "Mind Meld" as Star Trekkies might call it; "Synchronicity," as Carl Jung would describe it.

Who will finish my sentences? Who will finish hers?

∞

Letting go is the hardest thing in the world to do with a wife or a husband that you love, and harder still, that loves you. Studies show eighty-one percent of divorced men would seriously consider marrying the same person again. That seems high to me, but I do know quite a few clients, friends, and colleagues who have done so.

Would I marry her again? How can I? I'm still married to her in my heart and my stubborn head. Have I let go? Yes, to a certain extent. I'm afraid I will always feel married, if not to her, then to our past, and even to our non-existent future.

Yes, I acknowledge that all this could change in a heartbeat. After all, that was how quickly it seemed the divorce took place. One minute we're looking for houses to buy, the next we're looking for houses and apartments that will separate us, body and soul.

"Never say never," that's what they say. She saw me as I am—getting old, less energy, old knees being exchanged for titanium ones, arteries taken from legs to place in a rode-hard-and-put-up-wet heart, hair as gray as the old mare's, not to mention always needing and allowing each night to be a three dog night. Who is going to love a man like this, besides those three dogs lying on the bed with me? She would be rarer than chicken's teeth.

∞

Yep! It's that day! Feb. 14, – the made-up holiday for lovers everywhere. Unfortunately, or maybe fortunately, Hallmark doesn't make Valentine's Day cards for ex-husbands or ex-wives. Black roses are too hard to find, would cost too much to send, and in very bad taste of a sore loser.

But old dopey me will still send a text to her, saying I still love her because I do, because I can, though most would say it's not a great idea. But you see I do love her not for what she's doing or not doing, being with me, not wanting to be with me, but because she is still in my body, my blood, my bones, my psyche, dreams, and memory. And six months cannot make that go away. It may take years, maybe a lifetime. Divorce is a word with lots of power, but it is no great eraser of caring, concern, and kindness.

∞

Everyone's divorce is so different. I spoke with a former lover from thirty years ago and during that hour-long, impromptu, platonic phone call, she told me how she negotiated her divorce after twenty-eight years of marriage. She used a psychological technique known popularly as "Tapping" or EFT, and that is "what got me through; you should try it." She reports being essentially through the worst part in a few short months. I'm sure she

27

is because she thinks it so, "I think, therefore I am" says old Descartes. I think, no, I feel, it is going to take me longer because I am old school. While I may not cover the mirror for the rest of my life, or even wear a single black ribbon around my arm, my face, my body, my yearning for solitude and only occasional company says it all—I still mourn. I am bound to the grief process for as long as my own personal nature demands.

∞

Every morning I wake up in this strange house. I keep thinking soon I'll wake up from this dream/nightmare of divorce.

I drink my coffee and stare out the window and wonder how did this happen? I'm not a bad man, though I'd been one when I was young. She's not a bad woman, having never been bad, and if anything, having been too good.

We still love each other, and I don't know when we stopped "being in love." It wasn't a summer's day, perhaps the first of Spring, no, it couldn't have been in the spring because everyone is still in love when flowers are in bloom and the cold, chilly air has moved way north. I remember that summer before blackberries were about the only thing we kissed. Fall came, and one night we drove to the edge of the mountain and watched the under stars of the city below. Those were the last lights we saw; those were not the last tears we shed. That was many months ago—now.

But I still wake up, wipe the sleep from my eyes and think one day I'll really awaken. It is like the Taoist aphorism Chuang Tzu said, "I wake from dreaming that I was a butterfly and now I don't know if I'm a man who dreamt of being a butterfly or if I'm a butterfly who is dreaming he is a man."

∞

Yesterday I asked her if she was dating. She texted me, "no," she "wasn't," but did not want me to ever ask that question again, "please," she added.

I took this to mean many things. 1. It is none of my business. 2. Her boundaries are strong. 3. She is about to begin dating and has probably been thinking about it for a long while.

She said she couldn't be herself with me in the house we believe in, and so I took off my wedding ring and moved out.

She wanted to "move on" and would like it very much if I'd do the same so she could be "happy" for me and not have to see me sad and still grieving, and it would be great motivation for her to continue "moving on."

I told her "moving out" was the most I could accomplish at this time and that it took more energy than she could ever imagine.

You see, I don't want to move on. I want to time travel back ten or fifteen years ago and do things differently and be the husband I meant to be and be the husband she thought she was getting. I'd try to stop her from becoming the woman she became by giving her children instead of giving myself away to work and the road. But I can't go back and I can't move forward—not yet, not today, not tomorrow—she has her life in drive while mine is in park.

∞

Am I being disloyal to her by writing the most honest truth about our marriage and divorce as my memory and heart and hurt feelings will allow? I don't think so, because what I am saying is much more about me and my old misdemeanors. And I only share my experiences so I can better understand them, and if it helps one or a dozen readers, that's perfectly fine, but either way, I must take the poet Gerald Heard's advice: "He must go unprotected that he may be constantly changed."

I want to change and grow and know what I did wrong. Here is one thing I absolutely did wrong in the last two years of our marriage. My guilt and shame, mixed with my good egalitarian stance on gender, went too far once she became the primary breadwinner. I took on some, then all, of the domestic responsibilities. She worked, brought home the free-range, organic turkey bacon, and paid the bills while I shopped, did her laundry and mine, folded the clothes, washed the dishes, swept and vacuumed the floors, and made the bed. My age lowered my testosterone, increased my estrogen, and I got so tired and exhausted and angry I forgot to make love, was too tired for sex, not as interested, and not the man who used to come home from the gym or from working in the yard sweaty and semi-sexy.

In other words, we weren't equals, and I went from redneck, Southern macho to a redneck, college-educated, New Age, Men's Movement, recovery guy to be able to fill out a resume that would get me a full-time nanny job anywhere in this country or England.

I went too far down the guilt road for her having to work to exhaustion, when knowing all along she was raised to have servants and then be sexually serviced and delighted by a man who was an unapologetically hard, soft, unbridled, tender, torturer instead of an expert at filling the automatic dishwasher.

∞

Yesterday I made my first big decision without consulting with her. It was the first one I'd made from the bunker of solitude I call a house. I signed a book deal—my twenty-first. She was more objective and logical when it came to big decisions. She would have said I should have asked for a larger advance.

Truth is I still feel lost without her.

∞

I detest the word, or the two-letter word, description of myself and her: Ex-wife. Ex-husband. Ex-mother-in-law, Ex-father-in-law. Even this gets shortened to one letter because God knows how long it takes to write two: X. X-wife, X-husband. It is like X marks where the gold used to be but is no more. X is the kinder, gentler way of crossing out years and decades of meanings, magic, and manic behavior on both our parts.

X-lover, X-boyfriend, X-girlfriend. If some tragedy befell me and I had to find a better place for my animal companions to live, I wouldn't refer to them as my X-dog or, "how's my X-cat doing?"

But here I sit, my current dogs on the floor asleep, my cats at her house doing the same, writing in a journal about Ex's and X's, for there is nothing else to call our gone lovers. X says it all. Perhaps we should have a tattoo that says X on our arms or hands, like the scarlet letter Hester Prine had an embroidered, "A" for adultery; we should have an embroidered big black X to wear in public.

When we go to church or to social functions, they could say, "Okay, all you X's, you will meet in the basement of this building and remember, no wailing or gnashing of teeth; you'll disturb us 'currents.' We barely let you attend anyway, because you bring a portent of things to come to fifty percent of us who will join you."

∞

"Expression of speeches…is what is written or said. Forget not that silence is also expressive…"

Walt Whitman

It feels like I'm winding down the first half of this divorce journal trying to describe the emotional landscape of this foreign land called all alone.

We sign our first set of papers today. I asked if she was a hundred percent certain this is what she wanted. I wondered if I were the man I used to think I was and she needed me to be, would I scream at the top of my lungs, "No fucking way am I going to sign these papers!" But sign them I will. Who in their right mind would want to be with someone who doesn't have a shred of doubt after sixteen years that they are making the right decision?

∞

I am out in the wilderness, lost, but still wanting to believe I deserve better. Maybe I'm not meant for success in relationships, particularly matrimony, co-habitation. My track record, which can be found in my books, said I thrive in darkness like some old bat too beaten up to come out into the light.

Yes, I've had great loves in my life, but I seriously doubt any of them would count me among theirs.

So, I write, right after my heart is broken or after I push someone away. Did I push her away? Did I do enough to make her want to stay? Did I fight for her?

When we became romantically involved after about a year of friendship, my fears told me to run—that bad track record said run. She said, "No, you're not going to push me away. I'm going to fight for you. No one has ever fought for you before. Well, I'm going to. I love you and you love me. Now get your flying boy stuff straightened out; get into therapy again, but I'm not taking no for an answer," she said, standing in my darkly-lit hotel room in Miami all those long/short years ago.

Did I fight hard enough for her?

∞

"On this account the real man has to look his heart in the eye even when he is alone."

Confucius

It is a very different kind of loss that one negotiates at thirty or even forty. When I was younger and arrogant, I knew I wouldn't be alone for very long and so I could rest and revel in the empty time. I would read great poetry, write terrible poetry, and possibly get some prose worth printing. Then I'd break the chains in my platonic cave and go back into the world and look for another heart to break or have mine broken, and the circle would begin again. I'd be the Uboros, the snake chasing his own tail and making every effort to eat himself up while still alive.

This is different. This aloneness makes me want utter oblivion, the kind that comes with large doses of narcotics, bottles of booze, and the kind of sleep that Rip Van Winkle must have enjoyed buried under the chaos and hurt the world provides. I can't do even small doses of drugs, can't drink (I'm a recovering alcoholic of fifteen years), so I try to sleep as many hours as possible to silence the brain that keeps churning and yearning for God to

33

appear in a dream and explain what the fuck happened.

I don't sleep soundly for very long in the aloneness, so I get up early and read.

∞

"It is only when we can believe that we are creating the soul that life has any meaning, but when we can believe it...then there is nothing we do that is without meaning and nothing that we suffer that does not hold the seed of creation in it..."

May Sarton, *Journal of A Solitude*

I am beginning this year to scratch the surface of what the word "love" really means, and it doesn't mean what I thought it did before, or now after my marriage, has taken a nosedive off the highest mountain.

I got glimpses, like the time I was counseling a very intelligent, compassionate man. He was being honest about some terrible things he's said to his wife of twenty or so years.

I said, "Who on earth would you speak to like that?"

He paused and said, "You mean besides my wife? Maybe my children."

"In other words, you would never speak to your best friend that way or to an employee even? So why would you speak that way to the woman who has loved you, been there, given children to you, been with you through alcoholism and bankruptcy?"

"I guess because I can," he said, lowering his gaze to my studio's wooden floor.

I call it the "Best Friend Rule." If you wouldn't talk to anyone else harshly, in a belittling or shaming way, then why talk to your loved ones like that?

During the Pre-Divorce, and especially during this phase of the Divorce Door Closing, I tried really hard to remember for myself the Best Friend Rule when talking to or texting her.

It is a little easier to do, based on the fact that we were good friends before we married, and great best friends for many, many years. We told each other back then—even when being beaten up by bankruptcy and too much bourbon—that no matter what, should we split up, we'd end back up where we began—friends.

$$\infty$$

"Nobody sees a flower—really—it is so small—we haven't time
—and to see takes time like to have a friend takes time."

Georgia O'Keefe

I'm running out of things to say about the marriage that went out of business. Most of the tears have been shed and shared with people I love, though I've cried buckets full by myself in my mountain cottage.

My Ex is still just as friendly and gracious to me, though she has stopped sending emails, texts, and conversations with closings like "I love you" or "I miss you," and I have, too. Except on occasion, I feel my love for her, and I just get up and rip off a text or email, its content being, "I love and miss you," expecting nothing in return.

The delightful, disturbing dilemma I'm facing these last couple of weeks is due to—all of a sudden—being contacted by old high school, college, and graduate school sweethearts who, like me, are in their sixties, divorced, lonely, lovely, and very vibrant.

I receive their calls, texts, and emails with the gratitude of the poor, undernourished people who are thankful simply for a nourishing meal.

I am honored, touched, thankful, but like the dog who chases a car, what does he do with it when he catches it? He doesn't know. My heart is still sleeping in the bed beside my Ex, though my body and her body are far apart. For all I know, her body has already been comforted and connected to hopefully (if anyone) someone younger and more everything than me. That seems to be what she wanted except for the room and space to explore and implement her creativity.

Me, I just can't see being with anyone for a long, long time, if ever. Besides, my eccentricities, my beliefs, my being on the road, my political persuasion, my three dogs, my need for great periods of solitude, not to mention my bouts with depression and despair, reduces the pool of potential partners considerably.

∞

"Here there is nothing that does not see you. You must change your life."

Rilke

Divorce, like aging, demands that I change my life and so, since most of us are deeply afraid of change, we hold on to the familiar dog bone. The bone is dry, no meat, no taste, but we still hold on searching and sucking for the marrow. My former wife and I watched morning news for years. I turned it off after the divorce and haven't seen bad TV news in long time. The news of my own crash, my own war, my own less-than-great economy is all I can bear to watch for now.

I can hardly watch stupid television anymore. I'm kicking my one true banal addiction. In my hotel room in Pasadena this weekend where I was speaking, I didn't even turn it on. Trivia and banality and melodrama, not to mention reality shows, just seem silly compared to real loss, real attempts to be a "survivor" on this island inhabited by one.

I do try a little to mix and mingle—reaching out, for an introvert it's not easy, but Rilke says I must change. And while I'd rather have a sharp stick jabbed into my eye, I am trying to be social - well, a little more social.

I asked my dear friend Bill B., how does he meet so many people and know so many people? What was his secret to social success? He didn't take a second to answer, "Well, John, you begin by saying 'Hello.'" Wow, what a concept. As a socially anxious, divorced, introverted man, I never would have thought of it.

∞

Today and last night a little more anger finally appeared. I'd been wondering, was sadness the only feeling I'd have to feel and expel? I cried thirty, maybe sixty days or more, releasing the anguish of her decision to divorce.

But it came, not in a violent way, not in a thunderstorm, but just enough to feel, "Fuck you; I've had it. I'm done and you can go fuck yourself."

Knowing and believing what I believe, I did not call her and say these highly inappropriate things and never will. My anger took the form of two- and three-word texts to her when she'd tell what all I needed to do this weekend regarding our cats while she takes a trip to "see her parents," supposedly.

Those texts and emails were not punctuated with "Love you" or "Miss you," neither hers' nor mine, but merely "Thanks" or "Take care." For me, they were code for "Fuck you for kicking me to the curb, for falling out of love with me after all these years."

So, there it is—appropriate anger, appropriate language, since she'll never hear it or see it.

∞

Our first ceremony was performed in the fall woods that surround my cottage in Mentone on the mountain. Martín Prechtel, a Guatemalan shaman, wrapped us in a canary yellow and navy-blue wedding ceremonial blanket, and we stood with a dozen or more of my most intimate friends and entered into what he said was a sacred space.

The second marriage was performed the next day in the old historic Sally Howard Church that Colonel Howard built around a huge protrusion of rock the size of a small house that went inside the church building. It was rustic, without air conditioning. I asked a Unity minister who had trained with me to perform the ceremony attended by one hundred or so friends and family. Robert Bly was my best man and read poetry of our choosing from his book and a poem called *The Third Body*:

> *"...They obey a third body that they share in common.*
> *They have promised to love that body.*
> *Age may come; parting may come; death will come!*
> *A man and a woman sit near each other..."*

We went, after the wonderful reception, to Rome—Rome, Georgia, and for our wedding night stayed in a turn of the century renovated B&B, and the next day went to a county courthouse in Alpharetta, Georgia to get legally hitched by a Justice of the Peace.

We had three beautiful ceremonies, a hundred friends, a joyful reception, a wedding night in an old mansion and years of love, devotion, and finally a divorce.

∞

The last two days I've spent too much of my energy trying to explain to four old friends how the "perfect" marriage would end so abruptly. They were all shocked and concerned and truly in disbelief. "But you love each other so much!" "Do you think she'll recognize her mistake and want to come back in a year or two?" "Did you both see a marriage therapist?"

Good questions. I'm getting tired of answering them over and over.

Let me answer this question once and for all. We did everything that people who love each other are supposed to do - therapy, workshops, books, prayers. Very often, divorce has nothing to do with love.

We grew apart. She went from soft and tender to tough and tenacious. I went from high testosterone to low, to leader of the laundry room, author to a bottle washer, dog walker, to bone lonely.

She took one road; I took another, and she got "to divorce before me!"

∞

The grief came pouring out during and after my successfully attended webinar on grief. Then later, packing up the cats, who stayed with me while my ex was out of town, brought deep sobbing, the kind I hadn't done in several weeks.

Again, I know I've said this before but will again anyway: how do parents part with their children for a weekend, week, or month? Am I so fragile, so much more than others? But these paper-cut goodbyes and five- or one-word texts from her still cut, hurt, and make me bleed tears.

I'm about done with all of it! I'm tired of hurting, tired of writing about the hurt, tired of telling my friends about the hurt.

Is it time to just shut the fuck up and take my soul to the soul repair shop? I don't know where to go to be healed. Surly, not back to the friend I'd known for years and had lunch with Friday who listened to my whole tale of woe, and as we were walking out of Whole Foods said, "You are still very handsome, but you don't have that spark, that sparkle in your eyes that you always had. You carry yourself like an old man." It shocked me, so I didn't have a response until I was driving home, and I didn't have lunch with her again.

"I'm in pain, bitch! What am I supposed to look like? Did you hear a word I said? My family is broken; my wife is gone; my home is gone; my dreams have evaporated."

You have to watch who you pour your heart out to.

∞

I have grieved and written, grieved and written for ninety days. I took ninety days after the "D" word came out of her mouth and I began negotiating in shock, dismay, disbelief, and disappointment. It has been six months, one hundred and eighty days of absolute grief and sadness.

I've been more creative, more conversational, less introverted, less obsessed with TV, and read more than any time in recent memory. What does this second paragraph have to do with the first? Does it mean that the only time I get to be a real human is when I walk through the doorway of pain?

Can I only be creative in so far as I feel hurt, destroyed, rejected, reduced to a walking, talking mess?

I hurt, therefore I am. I am broken, therefore I am. I am lost; therefore, I find poetry. I am beaten, and therefore, I beg for forgiveness and write another book.

I have another one hundred and eighty days to go before I naively believe the grieving cycle will be complete. While it won't be as dramatic, traumatic, and painful as the first one hundred and eighty, there is still so much more to mourn. I hope I have the inner fortitude to finish the job before me.

∞

I feel like the proverbial snake shedding its skin. I have maybe half my old man skin lying behind me as I crawl forward, trying to go somewhere half in, half out. My first impulse is to stay here and wait, lie here passively until some passerby either reaches down and picks me up, pulls off the rest of my skin prematurely and discards it, or picks me up and cracks me like a whip and throws me to the side of the road to let nature finish the job of change, transition, and growth. If I lie here in this middle place, I will still fantasize that my former wife will come find me, pull the old skin back where it was, and everything will be as it was. Impossible! It is interesting to note that when crisis hits, change occurs, transitions abound, everyone naturally wants everything to go back to being the way it was. We want things to be normal again. Normal is a setting on a washing machine, and "Look Homeward Angel;" you can never go back to the way things were.

Her last layer of love for me has been shed, been shed a long time ago. She's moved forward and developed a very thick skin that will hopefully allow it to let the slings and arrows that are coming her way, shot by Fate's archer, like yesterday, which brought the sudden death of her brother-in-law.

No husband to drive her to the funeral. No husband to hold her at the gravesite. No husband to hold her hand and tell her it is going to be okay. Just an old snake slithering away in the opposite direction.

∞

"Suffering often feels like failure, but it is actually the door into growth. And growth does not cease to be painful at any age."

May Sarton

The flowers of love are more often watered with tears of sadness these days. You plant them and you wait, and you wait. They come up, we pull them up, put them in a vase or a pot ... We look at them, love them, and then they die. We do it all over again, except with perhaps a bit more patience and a little more appreciation while they are in the ground and we handle them with a little more tenderness as we uproot them into unnatural surroundings like the kitchen, the living room, or our office.

We wait all our life for the flowers that will not die, the love that never goes away. Last night, she came to visit me in a soul-shattering dream. We were arguing about her having a child and excluding me from the event, even naming the child "Indian" and a middle name I can't recall this morning. In the dream our dogs and cats ran free in the hospital while the doctor examined her only to find out that she had fluid on her knee and therefore could not conceive as she hoped.

When I woke, I knew it was my knee, my fluid, my pain that caused her infertility, her inability to embrace her destiny to be a mother because I was constantly on the road and returning home wearily, saying, "Next year I will cut back." That year never came or at least not in time.

This was a flower that died in her and me in real life far too many times before she acquiesced to Fate's fatal blow—a mother not to be and for me to answer Juan Ramon Jimenez's question from one if his best poems, "What have you done with the garden entrusted to you?"

∞

I felt it this past weekend—the slightest degree of further disconnect. I was in Massachusetts giving a lecture at the very church, the very podium that one of my heroes spoke at in the 1850s—Ralph Waldo Emerson. I was a kid who finally bought the candy store; it was my intellectual and spiritual Disneyland. I was delighted, bouncing up into the ether and flying into ecstasy.

On a practical level, I felt it because I knew I would not call her after the lecture like I'd done hundreds of times, but with much less enthusiasm, and share with her how it went.

I know it because she had a huge, complex presentation to give at work the day I would return, and she had not called or texted to get my support or suggestions.

Every week something happens, something gets said, something doesn't, that says to me I have to say, "Goodbye, I got to let you go." This is a phrase I've said to the living and the dying and had thousands of clients and workshop participants say with their outstretched hands pretending to hold on to someone they have never let go or at least not fully.

∞

It is not that my grief and mourning period is over or that I'm done. Indeed, in some ways, I've just begun another descent into this deep well. I'm not sure what comes next, but I get the feeling that the next phase is to be accompanied by a great deal of silence and solitude.

∞

Perhaps it's time to stop asking the most useless and unanswerable question that has ever been invented—"Why?" and just get on with the fact that she is gone, not coming back, and I still have more grieving to do, and keep putting one foot forward, and learn what people really mean when they say, "It's time to move forward, move on." The question that can be answered almost all the time with a little thought, support, information and insight is — "How?"

∞

"Perhaps the greatest gift we can give to another human being is detachment. Attachment, even when it imagines it is selfless, always lays some burden on the other person. How to learn to love in such a light, airy way that there is no burden." I would not learn this until much later."

May Sarton

Yesterday, my Ex and I ate lunch together for the first time in months. The whole family was there—Casper, Squeaky (who hid the entire time), Foxy, Luna, Bella, and me. For an hour or so, we were a family again.

We kept the conversation light until the very end when I said to her, "I want to be serious for just a few moments. Why did you marry me in the first place, other than because you loved me, and I loved you?"

She thought for a moment. "Because I thought, as an older man, you'd be able to watch me grow old and be more forgiving when I lost my looks and because you were so smart, creative, intelligent, and you made me laugh..." She said more, but it was sufficient.

It was gift enough that she spoke her truth, but the gift I'd like to give, aspire to give, is love from a distance and with a lightness and clean detachment that I've never managed before at the end of most all of my previous relationships.

∞

"Only connect. That was the whole of her sermon..."

E.M. Forster, *Howard's End*

Everyone at some time or another has been "bone tired." Today, I am that, but also, I am experiencing "bone loneliness." My Ex just texted me this morning that our beloved old cat Casper is sick, and at age nineteen or twenty, I must do my pre-grief work. How can a man miss a cat so much? My other cat, Miss Squeaky, is just as missed but in a different way. The bone loneliness is a culmination of one-part exhaustion, one-part illness and one-part physical pain.

Bone loneliness is present because the thought of one more loss this year will put me over some imaginary or real line that I'm afraid to cross because I might never come back.

∞

A soft spring rain is falling on this April morning. The crows are calling each other as I sit and experience the emotional hangover from an uncomfortable conversation I had yesterday with a friend of twenty-three years. He proceeded to tell me why my wife left me, a line he, or anyone else, should not cross. He barely knows her and knows only aspects of me, and little or nothing of our marriage.

It always strikes me as absurd that people want to weigh in on such personal matters when they have not been invited to do so. I asked my therapist, who has also been both of our therapist for many years, "Tell me what I did wrong." And I was grateful for the insight he provided. "Nothing," he said. "You both did everything you could. You are one of the most loving couples I've ever worked with in over thirty years. You just grew apart."

∞

When people first stagger into AA, beat-up, having beaten up others, lost, crazy, and scared, they are told by some old-timer that if they are really serious about getting and staying sober, they should attend ninety meetings in ninety days. The newbie looks like a drunk caught in the headlights of a police car when they hear it and can't conceive of it being a real possibility. I have written in this journal every day for ninety days straight plus regular entries several times a week now for six months, and like the newly sober Robert Frost said, "and miles to go before I sleep."

∞

With my former wife by my side, I felt like an aging phoenix that was able to rise again and again, even after my little death of a heart attack and triple bypass. I had to slow down and did so when my knees broke down and had to be replaced.

Rising physically, emotionally, and spiritually has not been easy or completely achieved, even now as I write. When I'd get ready to go off on a speaking tour, I would get nervous at best, and have an anxiety attack at worst. She would say, "Remember, even on your worst day, you're better than most other speakers. You'll do great!" It wasn't always true, but it meant the world to me to hear it.

Now, my assistant Kat, tries to do the same. She succeeds to a lesser degree but does provide some buoyancy and lift.

How much value was placed on such small, powerful things, such as words like, "Remember," "You'll be great!" How much we all forget, time and time again, things that were once fresh but have gotten overlaid by time and bad memory.

∞

"Like sudden blossoms on the naked trees, memories shoot; the place is all alive with questioning thoughts that like spring-guided bees find and bear back remembrance to my hive."

Julian Huxley, *The Old Home*

Yesterday, I drove my assistant down memory lane. I wanted her to see some of the pastoral beauty that surrounds our cottage, mine and Mrs. Former's cottage. We delighted in the apple blossoms that lined the road, the descent into Ireland-green pastures. As we drove over to Mountain Cove, Georgia to see an antebellum farm and have lunch, all I could remember were the times my wife and I drove these same roads, saw the same sights of dogwoods, smelled the scents that the extreme pastures were pushing into our glad nostrils.

Nostalgia is a terrible thing if the timing is not right. On yesterday's ride, while delightful because of Kat's enjoyment, I was still moody and bucolic, just as if the sun was hiding like it had been the two days prior. By the time we got back to the cottage, I was worn down and I slept for two hours, which helped only minimally. Bottom line: Memory Lane is a cul-de-sac that doesn't really go anywhere and must be driven at only the right time.

∞

"There is a field beyond wrongdoing and right doing. I'll meet you there."

Rumi

So, until now, all my entries have been really more about her letting me go, and about me trying to deal with the reality of what that means to be married for so long and to be divorced suddenly in my sixties. Now, like alcoholism, I must let her go, one day at a time. It's hard to believe I've stayed sober that way for fifteen years. I've thought about drinking several times. For some reason, the temptation has been stronger the last week or two than the first week or two after hearing the "D" word.

It has been nine months.

I talked, or should I say, I listened, to her last night for nearly an hour as she poured out the pain that had built up insider her about family issues, work, and much more.

This is how we started years ago—full circle—except we would allow each other equal time to tell our tales of conquests and woe. She had more need than I to talk, given I have Kat and a half-dozen other intimates with whom I can share my heart's torture.

I listened. She wanted a friend. I don't know how she handles so much stress and success at her work. Making lots of money doesn't seem to reduce the rush of life that comes at her like a Game of Thrones' dragon gone berserk.

I said something I shouldn't have to close the conversation, "Are you still sure divorce was the right thing?"

"It's the right thing. But you are my family; you will always be my family. I love you." And so, I go to bed sadder than I began the day—better friend, sad ex-husband.

∞

I don't think that I can endure another loss. Our precious, angry, overweight black cat, Squeaky, had to be put down by my Ex at the vet's office, and by me remotely, still shedding skin in Mentone.

She had been fine, and all of a sudden, stopped eating. The vet extensively examined her only to find she had been eaten up with cancer—lungs, liver, kidneys.

I say all of this because it hurts so deeply not to have been with my former wife to say our final goodbye to an essential, loving member of our family.

We negotiated the death of our precious cat like the loving couple we once were. For a few moments we had each other's backs, backed each other's decisions, didn't turn our backs on the other for a moment, though I have to admit I had a thought that lasted about fifteen seconds, "See, this is the life you chose—you wanted your space, your solitude, your freedom—now go do this by yourself." Thankfully, I remembered she and I were best friends; she and I are still friends, and she and I will always have some form of relationship for the rest of our lives. It is as she said, "We'll always be family. And now years later after our most miserable divorce we share love and joint custody of the three dogs she and I raised together. She gets them for a week and then I do. We talk often about our furry children and about work and our parents. She has a partner and I'm glad of this.

∞

It has been a long time now that I wrote these words to her: "I want to thank you for giving me this time for me to wrap my head and heart around this greatest loss. I am ready to let you go now. I love you so much. I don't want to hold you back...but I will always be there for you. We were once best friends, and you will always be family."

She said: "Thank you so much, honey. I'm incredibly touched and grateful for your words and the love behind them! Thank you for letting me go so lovingly and consciously. I will always be there for you."

∞

"Life will break you. Nobody can protect you from that, and living alone won't either, for solitude will also break you with its yearning. You have to love. You have to feel. It is the reason you are here on this earth. You are here to risk your heart. You are here to be swallowed up..."

Louise Erdrich

It is Spring on this mountain and as I take my three dogs on our daily walk in the woods, I try not to step on the small lavender flowers with petals smaller than the slenderest fingertip and as thin as an eyelash. As I walk, I think about how to end this book, and by now you know I know more about

50

loss and grief than I do about love. I wish I could tell you something about love that would be original, inspirational and moving. In his *Letters to A Young Poet*, Rilke tells the would-be poet he should never write poems about love because everything has already been said, and better, so all I'm going to do is tell you some things I know at this moment about Love, and with time maybe I'll learn some more.

∞

Love must always, whenever it is possible, exceed and trump need. We need to love the people we love more than need them. Yes, there will be times when need leaves love behind but ultimately it must not only catch up but win the race. When Ms. Former and I divorced I admit I needed her more than loved her for a long while. Now thanks to a miniscule level of maturity I've attained and with lots of time and tears, I love her more than I need her, but sometimes late at night I still "miss her laughter, her smiles and her mid-night sighs," to quote the poet Etheridge Knight.

∞

Most people, and I used to include myself, do not know the differences between detaching and distancing. I was a great distancer. When someone wronged me, perhaps just once, I banished them or I was "out of there." I stayed distant from almost everyone who even tried to be close to me until my thirties. That especially included the great and wonderful women who wanted to "just love" me.

∞

A good friend asked me the other day what is the difference. Detaching is done with love, best wishes, faith, and the feeling that I've done the right thing, and I know this by the gentle sleep I fall into at night after having done so. Disconnecting or distancing is always accompanied by some anger, resentment, regret, regression, and no one feels exactly good or right about it. With detachment there is a possibility of restitution, reuniting, and apologies that bring sweet forgiveness. Distancing provides infinite space and we fall into the black hole of depression or possibly despair and there is no opportunity for repair.

∞

I must learn how the men and women in my life want, need, and long to be shown love and then love them just that way. My former wife needed to go after sixteen years, and I had to let her by letting go and grieving which is the doorway to mature love. We have become the good friends we were when we first met in the Turks-Cacaos islands now over twenty years ago.

∞

I must learn to let those who love me do so in the way they can now that my hunger and thirst for unconditional love has subsided as my youth has given way to my adulthood. I have to find a way to let the sweet honey of their friendships enter my heart for the time I have left.

∞

Rumi says, "Your task is not to seek love but merely to seek and find all the barriers within yourself that you have built against it." With that most true teaching I have to let go of looking outward for the happiness or hope that some woman will waltz into this solitary life and tolerate the three dogs that go to bed with me every night and the other several dozen idiosyncrasies that I wake up with every morning.

∞

In order to truly love others and myself I must at this stage of my life accept my own inner lover, who, as Kabir says, "Why such a rush?" and take my time to learn to listen to that voice inside me that will whisper or yell the old Arabic proverb—"Haste is of the devil. Slowness is of God." I must go gently and patiently in the direction of love and loving.

∞

Finally, I must commit to continue on this journey to Unbecome the young, brash, sometimes arrogant young man who thought he knew a lot more than he really did, which is equally hard to do as it was to say goodbye to a marriage and the dreams that accompanied it. As a child I came into this world reluctantly according to my mother's tale of a painful twenty-four-hour delivery just to BE here instead of always trying to become something or somebody.

∞

John Lee

John Lee, MA — teacher, trainer and life coach — is a pioneer in the fields of self-help, anger, co-dependency, creativity, recovery, relationships and men's issues. In the mental health field, he is considered the therapist's therapist and regularly trains and mentors therapists on how to work with clients and how to work on themselves. He has taught his techniques and theories to thousands of individuals, couples, families, groups, corporations, and therapists all over the world.

Lee has given keynotes at over three hundred professional conferences and provided training for therapists in a number of professional settings. He has done numerous readings at colleges and universities and has even read his poetry at the Library of Congress.

Work with John Lee in person or from the comfort and convenience of your own home or office in 50-minute sessions via phone, FaceTime, Skype, Zoom, etc.

For deeper exploration of issues with a lot of time devoted to solutions — something the traditional 50-minute session cannot provide, schedule a 1- or 2-day Intensive.

To schedule a session, 1- or 2-day Intensive or to bring JOHN to your treatment facility, community group, or place of worship:

Contact: john@johnleebooks.com, assistant@johnleebooks.com, or visit the website www.johnleebooks.com.

Books Published

The Flying Boy Letters: Getting Back to Y'all All 30 Years Later. Teitelbaum Publishing, 2019.

Breaking the Mother-Son Dynamic: Resetting the Pattern of a Man's Life and Loves. Health Communications, Inc. 2015.

The Half-Lived Life: Overcoming Passivity and Rediscovering Your Authentic Self. Lyon's Press, 2011.

Emotional Intelligence for Couples: Simple Ways to Increase the Communication in Your Relationship. Turner Publishing, 2011.

The Anger Solution: The Proven Method for Achieving Calm and Developing Healthy, Long-Lasting Relationships. DaCapo Lifelong Books, 2009.

When the Buddha Met Bubba. Turner Publishing, 2009.

The Missing Peace: Solving the Anger Problem for Alcoholics/Addicts and Those Who Love Them. Health Communications, Inc., 2006.

The Secret Place of Thunder: The Poetry & Prose of Knowing. Woodstock: Monarch Publishing Associates, 2004.

Courting a Woman's Soul: Going Deeper into Loving and Being Loved. Monarch Publishing Associates, 2003.

Growing Yourself Back Up: Understanding Emotional Regression. Three Rivers Press, 2001.

The Flying Boy Book III: Stepping Into the Mystery. Honey Creek Publishing, 1997.

Writing from The Body: For Writers, Artists, and Dreamers Who Long to Free Their Voice. St. Martin's Press, 1994.

The Dragon's Letters. Ally Press, 1995.

Too Much Talk or Too Little. Honey Creek Publishing, 1994.

A Quiet Strength: Meditations on the Masculine Soul. New York: Bantam, 1994.

Facing The Fire: Experiencing and Expressing Anger Appropriately. Bantam, 1992.

At My Father's Wedding. New York: Bantam, 1991.

> Hardcover Book of the Month Club and Quality Paperback Books. Has been translated into German, French, and released in a U.K. version.

Recovery: Plain and Simple. Health Communications, Inc., 1990.

The Flying Boy Book II: The Journey Continues. Health Communications, Inc., 1989. Translated into Spanish.

The Flying Boy: Healing The Wounded Man. Health Communications, Inc., 1987.

> Listed as a best seller by Publishers Weekly. *The Flying Boy* has been translated into Chinese, Japanese, Dutch, Greek and Spanish. Sold movie rights.